ST JOHN'S PILG
BEVERLEY MINS
BRIDLINGTON

There was a tradition in the Middle Ages for pilgrims to visit both the shrines of St John of Beverley and St John of Bridlington. Indeed, in 1481 Henry V gave thanks to both saints after the Battle of Agincourt.

Our pilgrim route from Beverley to Bridlington is not authenticated by contemporary evidence because there is very little and maps with roads on were not available until the seventeenth century. However we do know that pilgrims walked a route similar to ours, stopping on the way to visit churches, as we did, for prayer and hospitality. It is not inconceivable that they, too, read passages of St Augustine on their journey. We arrived at the Augustinian Priory of St Mary, Bridlington on the 28th August 2013, St Augustine's Day, to celebrate the 900th anniversary of its foundation in 1113.

Beverley Minster was built in the period 1220-1425. Like Bridlington Priory it contains elements of three Gothic styles: Early English, Decorated and Perpendicular, but, unlike the Priory, where a great deal of Early English work was destroyed at the Dissolution in 1539, the Minster has a magnificent Early English East end. Beverley was a wealthy church because of pilgrims visiting the tomb of St John and because of the wool trade. It was spared at the Dissolution when Beverley grandees agreed to buy the building for £100.

St John of Beverley may have been born at Harpham. He certainly was Bishop of Hexham (687-706) and of York (706-714) and is thought to have retired to a monastery where he died in 721.

In 1037 he was canonised by the Pope for his holy life and evidence of miracles after his death. The order of St John and that of St John of Bridlington were abolished by Henry VIII who destroyed the shrines. However in 1664 the bones of St John of Beverley were discovered and reinterred between the nave and the choir stalls. Bridlington Priory was founded in 1113 by the Augustinians on the site of a pre-conquest church. Existing buildings were probably used until the civil war between Stephen and Matilda ceased in 1154. The earliest remnants we have, the cloisters in the north aisle, are from the late 12th century. In the early 1200's building began in earnest, working down the north aisle and to the east end in the Early English style. Much of this was destroyed at the Dissolution. A wonderful nave in the Decorated style was probably completed in the 1300's and finally in the 1400's the magnificent West end. Like Beverley Minster, the Priory was very wealthy and many pilgrims came to the shrine of St John of Bridlington. More wealth was gained from the wool trade.

St John of Bridlington was born in 1319 in Thwing near Bridlington. He studied at Oxford and then returned to the Priory as a canon before being made Prior. He died in office in 1379. Even in his lifetime he enjoyed a reputation for miraculous powers and holiness. He was canonised in 1401, the last saint before the English Reformation. Many pilgrims, including Henry V, visited the shrine and fishermen and seamen testified to his saving powers. In addition to abolishing the order of St John of Bridlington and his shrine, Henry VIII also destroyed the east end of the Priory and all the monastic buildings at the Dissolution in 1539.

BRIDLINGTON

Kilham

Lowthorpe

Harpham

DRIFFIELD

Nafferton

Skerne

Hutton

North Sea

Kilnwick

Watton

Lockington

Scorborough

Arram

Molescroft

BEVERLEY

HULL

ALTERNATIVE ROUTE
VIA WOLDGATE
Kilham to Priory   7½ miles

INTRODUCTION
THE PILGRIMAGE FROM BEVERLEY MINSTER TO THE PRIORY CHURCH OF ST MARY, BRIDLINGTON IN CELEBRATION OF 900 YEARS OF THE PRIORY CHURCH

This Pilgrimage was conceived by the PRIORY WALKING GROUP to celebrate the 900th Anniversary of the founding of the Priory Church of St Mary, Bridlington. The route was planned by three of the group's walkers over a period of three years, each walker being responsible for one third of the walk. The walk started at the North Door of Beverley Minster on the fourth Monday in August 2013, and was walked over three stages arriving at the Priory late on Wednesday afternoon, to join in a celebration service in the Church on St Augustine's Day, 28th August. The full distance of the walk covers 36 miles on well defined paths and quiet country lanes. The route was compiled by linking the Minster Way (as far as the village of Kilnwick) with public rights of way to reach our destination. It is, we think, the route, or part of it, which St John of Bridlington took on one of his pilgrimages from Beverley to Bridlington.

To any one who is interested in history or architecture, Beverley is the place to be, the Minster being one of the finest churches in the North. It took 250 years to build, having been started in the 13th century. Butcher Row, Toll Gavel, and Wednesday and Saturday Markets are virtually free of traffic, allowing a nice start to the walk. St Mary's Church post-dates the Minster by around 100 years. Note the beautiful wrought iron gates. If you go into the Church, look for the White Rabbit which is said to have been the inspiration for the rabbit in Lewis Caroll's Alice in Wonderland.

Beverley, at one time, had five Town Gates, the North Bar, built in 1409, is the only one remaining. Look for the plaque on the wall giving the cost of construction. Now begin a quiet stroll through this lovely town until reaching the by-pass, then stride out along the lanes and paths to reach your destination.

ROUTE TAKEN
miles

BEVERLEY MINSTER – Molescroft By Pass – Leconfield Low Park – Arram	4
ARRAM – Scorborough Gate House – Scorborough Village (Church) – Lockington	4¾
LOCKINGTON (Church) – Kilnwick (Church) – Cawkeld – Watton (Church & Abbey)	4½
WATTON ABBEY – Hutton Cranswick- Hutton (Church)	3½
HUTTON – Skerne Bridge – Skerne Village (Church) – Bell Mills	3¼
BELL MILLS – Driffield (Church) – Meadow Lane	1
DRIFFIELD – Meadow Lane – Markham Lane – Nafferton (Church)	2
NAFFERTON – Lowthorpe (Church) – Harpham (Church)	3
HARPHAM – Kilham (Church)	3
KILHAM to BOYNTON	6
BOYNTON (Church) – PRIORY CHURCH	2½
	TOTAL = 37½

FIRST LEG OF PILGRIMAGE
BEVERLEY MINSTER TO WATTON

Distance: 13 miles

Beverley is a large Market town, steeped in history and architecture. The Minster is one of its premier attractions. Started in the 13th Century it took 250 years to build. The walk starts from the North Door of the Minster. Walk straight ahead along Highgate, to a pedestrian crossing which crosses Lord Robert's Road to lead you into Wednesday Market and along Butcher Row (which is pedestrianised,) curving left past Wilbert Lane and Watergate leading into Toll Gavel and then Saturday Market (the larger of the two markets) passing the Market Cross on your right. Continue straight ahead and look out for St Mary's Church to your right. You are now on North Bar Within. Passing through the small arch of North Bar, the only one of Beverley's five gates still in existence, note the plaque on the wall, and then admire the beautiful wood carvings on the buildings at the opposite side. Continue past Wylies Road and into North Bar Without, keeping a look out for more carving above the doors of the fine properties which flank this road. These depict the trade of the tenant at the time of building. As you pass the Sessions House on the left, cross over the road onto New Walk with its magnificent horse chestnut trees. Pass the end of Bainton Close to arrive at three concrete posts set in the footpath. **(1 Mile)**

At this point, turn right into Bleach Yard Lane, passing the Cemetery on your left. Negotiate two metal kissing gates and continue ahead along this lane, between properties, emerging at the Molescroft sign on the wall to your left, turn to your left along Woodhall Way. Follow the footpath for 250 yards then cross the road into Scrubwood Lane. 20 yards on turn left into Oaktree Drive, turning left onto a narrow path between gardens (with a waymark post) after No 29.

Stay on this path, past the end of Alpha Avenue, to reach a high wooden fence on your left. Walk straight ahead on a tarmac path to an estate road, follow this left for 20 yards then curve right on the roadside footpath to a small roundabout. Continue ahead until meeting the former Beverley/Market Weighton Railway line (now a walking route called "Hudson Way".) Cross over the old rail line continuing for a further 150 yards to arrive at the "The Hayride" pub. Keeping the pub to your left, walk through the pub yard to emerge on to the Beverley North Eastern by-pass. **(2 Miles)**

St Mary's, Beverley

St Mary's was founded as a Norman Church in 1120, and was completed over the next 400 years incorporating some of the finest architecture in Britain, containing many interesting features. It is said to have provided the inspiration for Lewis Caroll's White Rabbit in Alice in Wonderland, a carving of which can be found in the Church. A visit is very worth while if time permits.

"The Hayride"

Disused Railway

North Bar

St Mary's Church

BEVERLEY

START

The Minster

| BEVERLEY MINSTER to |
| BY-PASS   2 Miles |

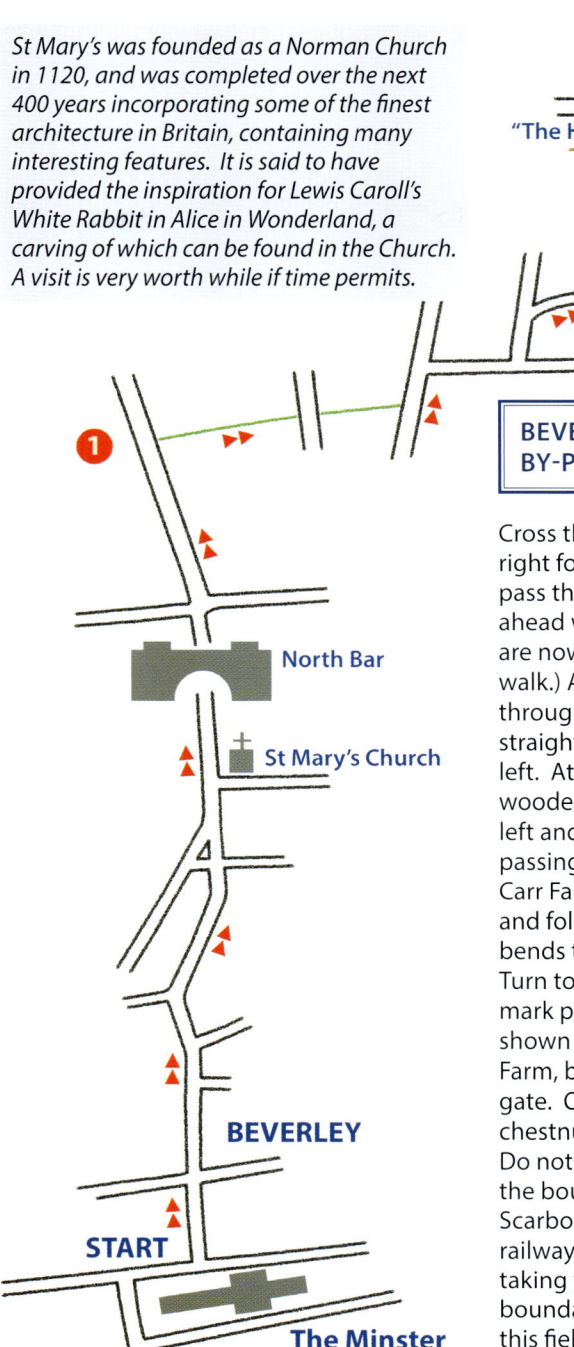

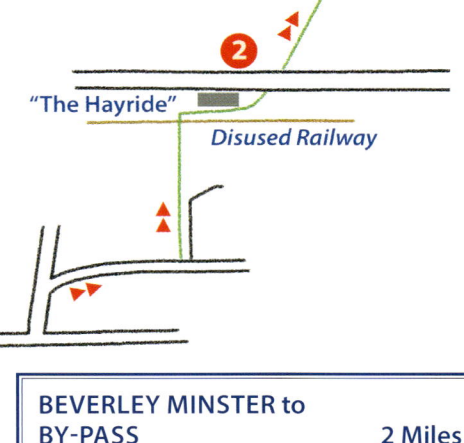

Cross the road with great care, walk to your right for 30 yards to a small kissing gate, pass through this gate and walk straight ahead with the hedge to your right. (You are now in the country for the rest of your walk.) At the end of this field "dog leg" right, through a gap in the hedge, continuing straight ahead with the hedge now on your left. At the end of this field, pass through a wooden kissing gate and turn immediately left and walk for approximately 100 yards, passing a farm to your right (Molescroft Carr Farm). Walk to a tarmac farm road, and follow this for 30 yards to where it bends to the left, near a war-time pillbox. Turn to your right, following the way-mark post (laid in the hedge) to a house shown on the map as Leconfield Low Park Farm, but signed "The Chestnuts" at the gate. On reaching the farm look out for a chestnut tree, and here turn to your right. Do not enter the farm, but continue along the boundary hedge to meet the Hull to Scarborough railway line, where an old railway sleeper crosses a ditch to your left taking you into a field. Follow the railway boundary on your right to the far end of this field to a stile, go over the stile and stay alongside the railway. **(3 Miles)**

BY-PASS to SCORBOROUGH GATEHOUSE
4 Miles

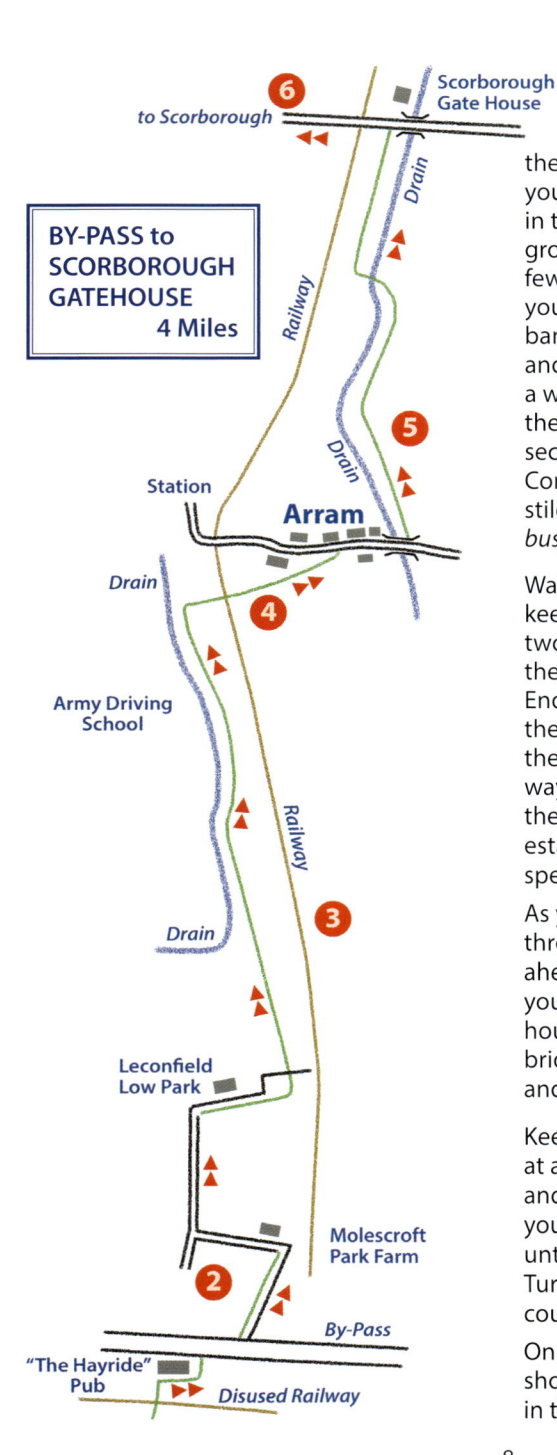

After approximately 500 yards the gap between the railway and the water course widens, at this point follow the water course to your left. Notice, to your left, the mounds of earth and tracks in the far fields. These are the training grounds for the Army Driving School. A few yards after passing a metal gate to your left, you come to a stile. Stay on the bank top, which veers slightly to the left, and continue until you arrive at a stile over a wooden fence to your right, cross over the stile and walk straight ahead to the second stile approximately 70 yards ahead. Continue over this stile to cross two more stiles over the railway line. *(This is a very busy line, Please Cross With Care.)* **(4 Miles)**

Walk towards the field corner ahead keeping the fence to your left, cross over two more stiles and turn left onto a track, then right onto a road which leads to Beck End Farm. Walk straight ahead keeping the farm buildings to your left and go over the bridge, turn immediately left at the way-mark sign to follow the bank top with the drain to your left, passing many newly established lakes, which attract many species of birds and other wild life.

As you come to a concrete bridge, go through the kissing gate keeping straight ahead with the drain still to your left until you come to a large complex of glass houses on the far bank and a second bridge. Go through the two kissing gates and over the road. **(5 Miles)**

Keep following the bank top as you arrive at a third bridge, turn left over the bridge and then right to follow the drain, now to your right, with the rail line to your left, until reaching Scorborough Gate House, Turn left over the rail crossing to follow the country lane to Scorborough village.

On a clear day look to your left and you should get a good view of Beverley Minster in the distance. **(6 Miles)**

St Leonards Estate Church was rebuilt for the Hotham Family by John Loughborough Pearson in 1859. A notable ex-resident of Scorborough, it was Sir John Hotham who closed the gates of Hull to King Charles the First.

Scorborough Church

As you enter Scorborough it is very worthwhile to visit this beautiful Church.

(7 Miles)

Make your way through this village, cross over the busy Beverley to Driffield road with care onto a large lay-by. Follow this road as it bends right and on the left, go through a small hand gate at the side of a farm gate to cross the paddock at 1 o'clock to the far left hand corner then go through a second hand gate. Cross over the farm road, keep the electric pole to your right and follow the way-mark post indicating 'Minster Way' straight ahead. Follow the well defined path across this arable field to reach a concrete farm road, cross over the road and follow the headland keeping the hedge to your left to reach another way-mark post indicating a left turn on to a path over a second arable field. Here follow the defined path across the field to the far hedge, turning right and keeping the hedge to your left head for the trees. As you reach the corner of the field turn right for approximately 10 yards then left over a wooden bridge to cross a dyke. Continue straight ahead to follow the well defined path over the arable fields to reach a wooden bridge with hand rails at the side of the wood. Cross the bridge and follow the path through the trees to reach a five bar gate leading out of the wood. Go through this gate and continue straight ahead across the rough grass meadow keeping the dyke to your right.

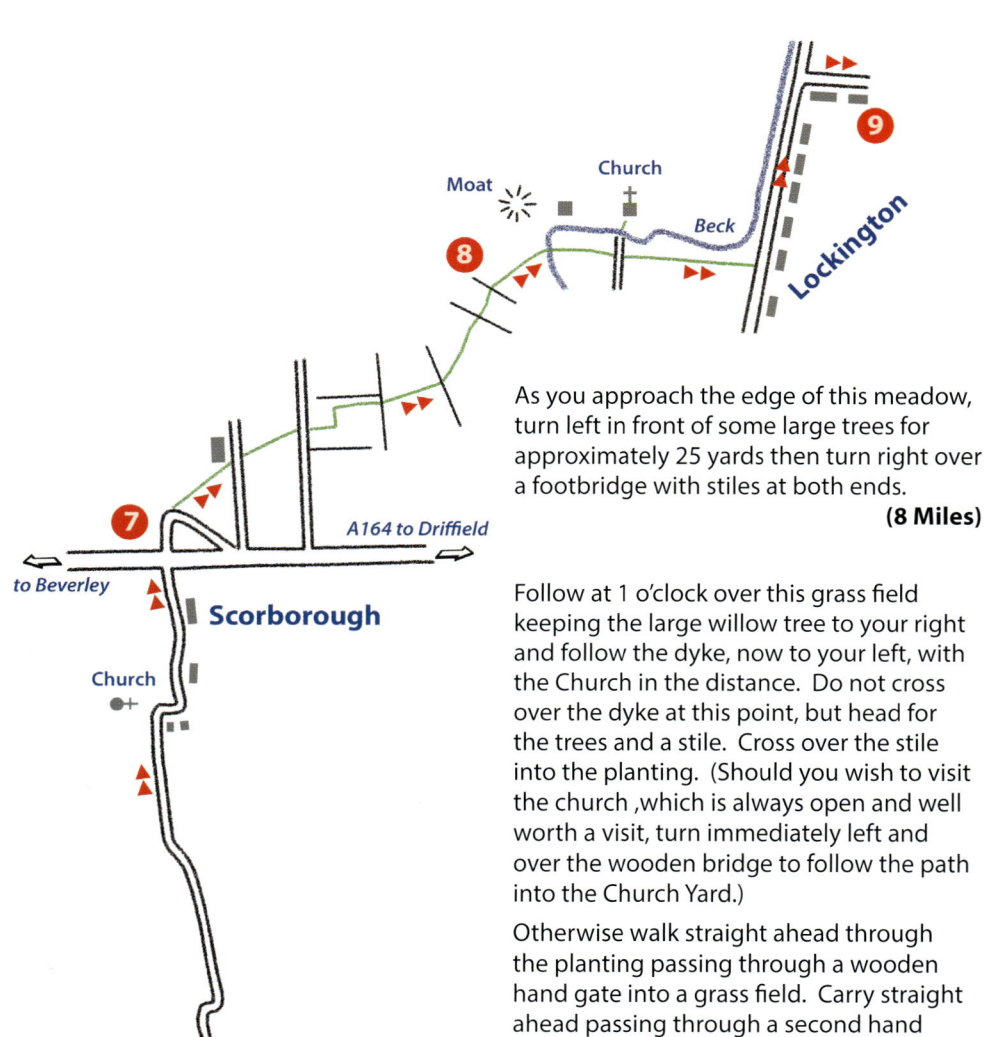

As you approach the edge of this meadow, turn left in front of some large trees for approximately 25 yards then turn right over a footbridge with stiles at both ends.
(8 Miles)

Follow at 1 o'clock over this grass field keeping the large willow tree to your right and follow the dyke, now to your left, with the Church in the distance. Do not cross over the dyke at this point, but head for the trees and a stile. Cross over the stile into the planting. (Should you wish to visit the church ,which is always open and well worth a visit, turn immediately left and over the wooden bridge to follow the path into the Church Yard.)

Otherwise walk straight ahead through the planting passing through a wooden hand gate into a grass field. Carry straight ahead passing through a second hand gate within the fence and continue straight ahead and over the wooden bridge with a single hand rail. Crossing over a dyke head towards a small hand gate, go through the gate and follow the path leading between the houses to emerge on to the village street. Turn left, keeping the stream to your left until arriving at the road junction on your right, indicating a right turn, towards Kilnwick. Turn right along this quiet road with its wide grass verges as you leave the village. **(9 Miles)**

SCORBOROUGH GATE HOUSE to LOCKINGTON   3 Miles

St Mary's Church, Lockington

St Mary's Church, Lockington was originally built in 1150 by the Norman Lord of the Manor. The Nave and Chancel were extended in 1330, the side chapel being added in 1340. The nave was altered when the Norman door was blocked up and a gallery built at the west end. Major overall restoration was carried out in 1893 by Temple Moore.

After approximately ½ mile turn right at the 'T' Junction. After about 200 yards, turn left (signed Kilnwick) onto a second quiet road which leads you into the village of Kilnwick, (approximately 1 mile) at the cross roads.

(10 Miles)

Walk straight ahead into Church Lane arriving at All Saints' Church. (Another Church well worth visiting.)

Where the road bends right, take the wide grass track to your left with a bungalow to the right, signed Minster Way.

Continue straight ahead through a metal five bar gate and over a dyke. (Way-mark post indicating right 1¾ miles to Watton village.) DO NOT turn right here, but follow the sign 'Minster Way' straight ahead, making for the metal kissing gate and bridge over the dyke in the far hedge. Having passed through this gate, leave the Minster Way as it bears left into the corner of the wood. We walk straight to the far side of the field, to pass through a wide opening in the hedge with a way-mark arrow. Go through this opening and head at 2 o'clock making for the far corner of the field, cross over a wooden bridge with two stiles. Walk straight ahead to a way-mark in the hedge turning right and walk with the hedge to your left, passing through a metal farm gate.

(11 Miles)

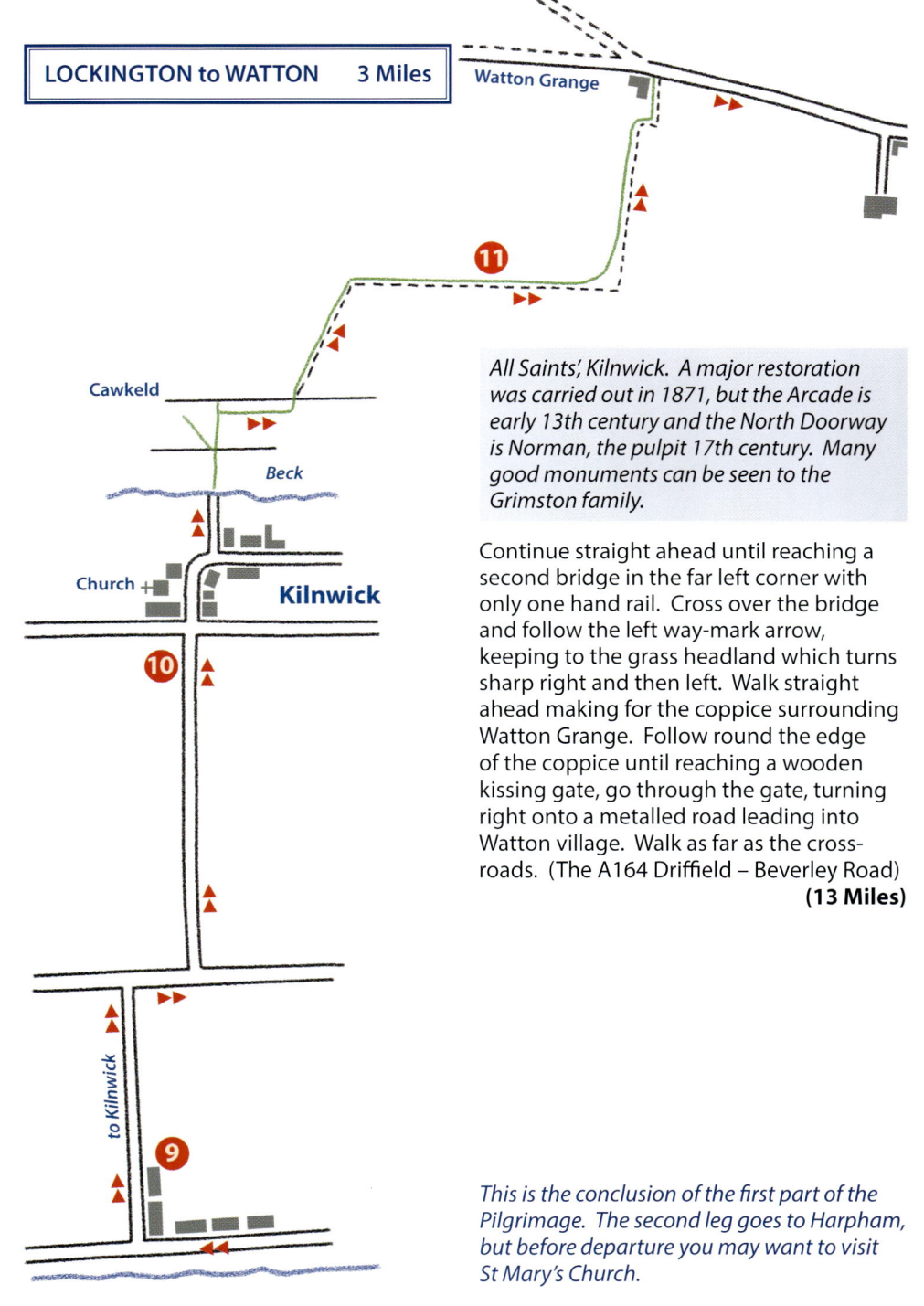

LOCKINGTON to WATTON   3 Miles

Watton Grange

⑪

Cawkeld

Beck

Church

Kilnwick

⑩

to Kilnwick

⑨

All Saints', Kilnwick. A major restoration was carried out in 1871, but the Arcade is early 13th century and the North Doorway is Norman, the pulpit 17th century. Many good monuments can be seen to the Grimston family.

Continue straight ahead until reaching a second bridge in the far left corner with only one hand rail. Cross over the bridge and follow the left way-mark arrow, keeping to the grass headland which turns sharp right and then left. Walk straight ahead making for the coppice surrounding Watton Grange. Follow round the edge of the coppice until reaching a wooden kissing gate, go through the gate, turning right onto a metalled road leading into Watton village. Walk as far as the cross-roads. (The A164 Driffield – Beverley Road) **(13 Miles)**

This is the conclusion of the first part of the Pilgrimage. The second leg goes to Harpham, but before departure you may want to visit St Mary's Church.

All Saints', Kilnwick

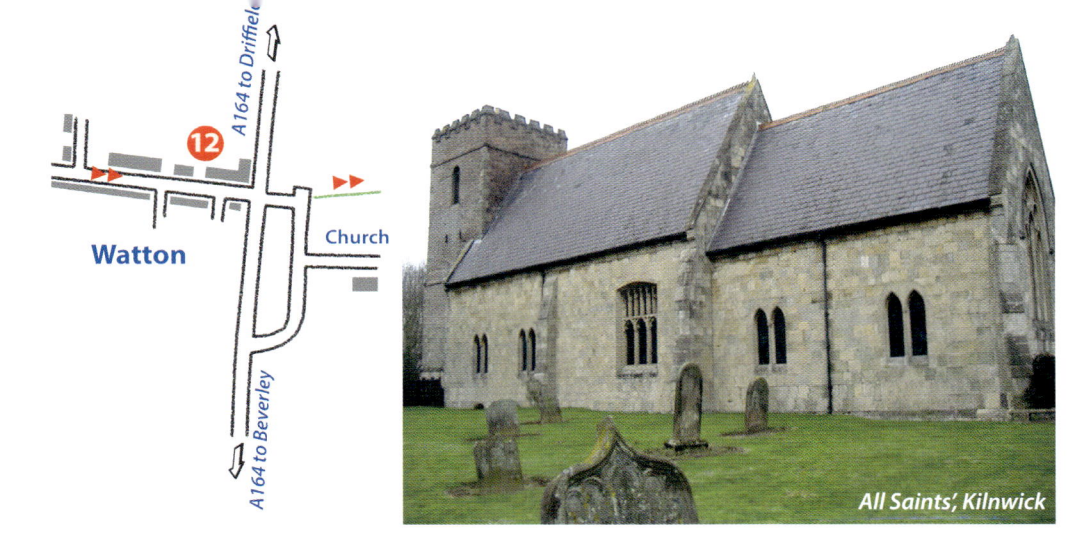

SECOND LEG OF PILGRIMAGE
WATTON TO HARPHAM

Distance: 12¾ miles

If you are visiting the Church, cross over the A164 to the small lay-by and walk straight ahead along the path in an easterly direction between the two hedges until reaching a metal kissing gate (one of many.) Go through this gate and head across the paddock at 2 o'clock to reach the entrance to the Church.

Having visited the church, back track to the kissing gate and turn right, heading for the derelict building ahead. Keep to the left of the building and you will arrive at two more metal gates. Turn left and walk straight ahead in a northerly direction through pastures towards Hutton Cranswick following the way-mark sign to reach a fourth metal gate. Keep straight ahead passing through two more metal gates with a track to Abbey Farm between. Continue ahead as per the way-mark, following the headland to reach another metal gate. At the far end of this field cross over the dyke and through a metal gate passing through a 'dog leg' to your right. Turn left at the three way directional way-mark signs. After 20 yards turn right over a wooden footbridge following way-mark sign "Cranswick ½ mile" straight ahead to a small wooden hand gate. Continue ahead keeping the hedge and ditch to your right until reaching a rough farm track, walk straight ahead and pass through another metal kissing gate. Keeping the house to your right, follow the way-mark sign 'Cranswick' along this road for a short distance until reaching a gap in the left hand hedge. Turn left and cross over two stiles as per the way-mark arrows. Follow the path at 1 o'clock heading for a metal gate in the far corner. Turn right through the hedge passing a 3rd stile and into a grass field, follow the path to your left until you reach another stile. Go over the stile and follow the narrow path between the fence on the left and hedge on the right until emerging between houses onto the road surrounding the village green. Cross the green at 11 o'clock to reach the main street, turn left. **(16 Miles)**

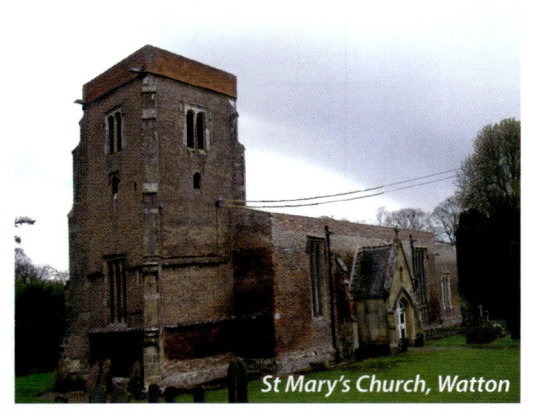

Having crossed over the village green, follow the signed path opposite the War Memorial, between the Post Office and the White Horse Inn. Walk straight ahead to where the path leads through a large bramble patch. Follow this path to the end turning left on a small wooden bridge over a dyke and through the metal kissing gate. Go straight ahead to pass through a second kissing gate, walk straight ahead with the hedge to your left. At the end of this hedge go through another wooden kissing gate and head, on a well defined path, for the

St Mary's Church, Watton

WATTON to CRANSWICK

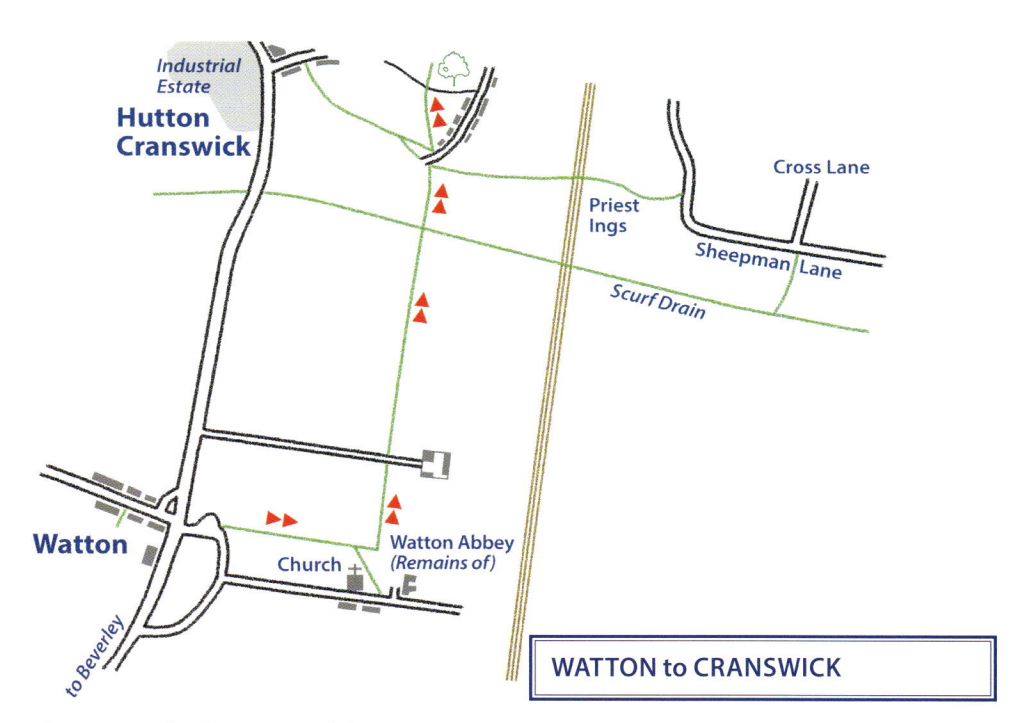

planting in the far corner of the field. Enter the new planting, which is a Nature Conservation Area known as Century Wood, keep to the right where the path forks, before emerging onto the Cranswick-Hutton road. Turn right onto the road, keep straight ahead at the junction and then fork left to St Peter's Church, Hutton. This is a beautiful, well kept Church well worth a visit.

On leaving the Church, take the path as signed across the grave-yard at the East End of the church, pass through a metal kissing gate to your right. Follow along this cinder track until reaching the main road. Turn to your left and follow the road as it bends slightly to the right. Before you get to the railway crossing there is a road (Orchard Lane) on your left, follow this road for a short distance until you see a footpath sign on your right. Take the path across the field to the railway crossing. Cross carefully and follow the railway line for approximately 200yds turning right alongside a beck to your left. Stay on this path until you reach the Cranswick – Skerne road.

St Peter's Church, Hutton

St Peter's has an early English Nave and Chancel, but the south doorway is Norman and the Tower 15th century.

War Memorial, Cranswick

Skerne Grange

As you reach the Cranswick-Skerne road, turn to your left and walk along the road for approximately one mile, until you come to a footpath sign on the left. Follow this path past Skerne Grange, to meet the Skerne-Driffield road, and turn to your left. Keep to this road for a further half mile until there is a footpath sign to your right to Skerne Hill. Follow this track, and, as you approach the first building, veer left to go behind it. Walking past a couple of buildings you come into a field with a hedge on your left. Walk along the path at the side of the field until you reach a gap in the hedge, turn left and cross the field back to the Skerne-Driffield road. Turn right and continue along the road passing Bell Mills to reach the railway crossing. At the main road turn right and follow the main street through Driffield.

Map of Hutton showing: to Driffield, Elm Tree Farm, Mill Street Farm, Church, Hutton Gatehouse, Skerne Bridge, to Skerne, Megginsons Turnpike, Rech Grd, Hutton, Hutton Balk, Windmill, Hutton Chalk Pit (dis), Manor Farm, Nursery, West Field Megginsons Bridge.

All Saints Church, Driffield, has a splendid 15th century tower. In 1880 George Gilbert Scott carried out a considerable restoration and rebuilding, the church has a Norman Font and a large collection of Mediaeval sculptures.

Outside on the East wall is a carving of a Bishop, believed to be Paulinus the great missionary and first Archbishop of York.

HUTTON

Walk along the main street passing the railway station on your right and the EYMS Bus depot. Keep straight ahead through the traffic lights passing the Methodist Church to your left. At the next turning left, All Saints', the Parish Church of Driffield, stands to your right.

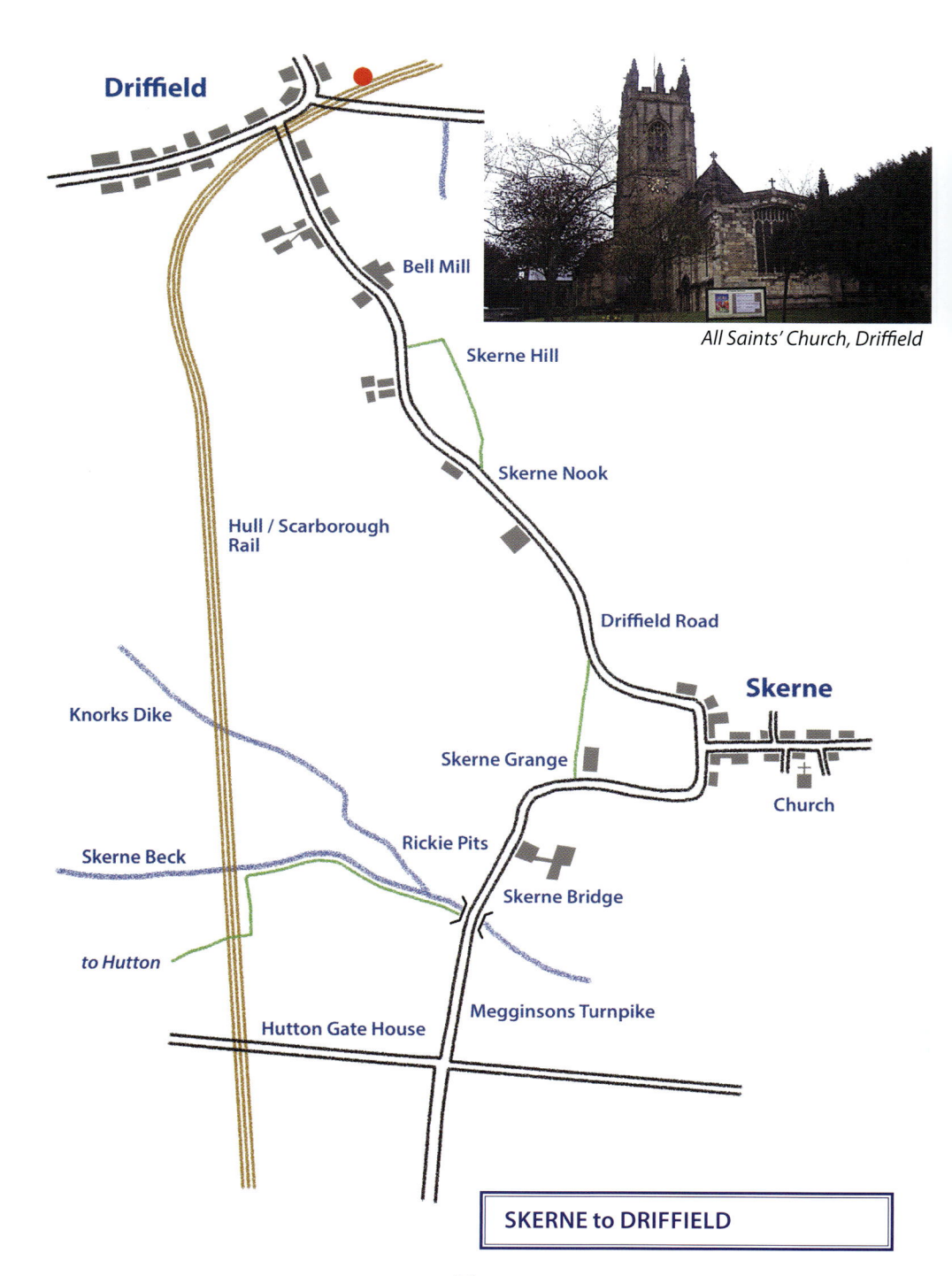

Driffield

Bell Mill

Skerne Hill

Skerne Nook

Hull / Scarborough Rail

Driffield Road

Skerne

Knorks Dike

Skerne Grange

Church

Skerne Beck

Rickie Pits

to Hutton

Skerne Bridge

Hutton Gate House

Megginsons Turnpike

All Saints' Church, Driffield

SKERNE to DRIFFIELD

Canal Head, Driffield

Retrace your steps to the railway station turning left over the lines and along past the Riverhead, and the old trading dock of the Driffield Canal.

Carry on to the B1249 Driffield-Wansford road. Cross over and walk down Meadow Road. Keep on where it turns into a track until you again reach the Hull – Scarborough railway line. Cross over the line carefully and keep on the path through the trees before a left/right dog leg, joining the minor road from Nafferton to Driffield.

All Saints' is an outstanding church building, having a restored Chancel Arch which is Norman, but the Chancel itself with the south Aisle and Arcade are Decorated Perpendicular along with the Tower, north Arcade and Clerestory. The font is Norman and the nave roof 17th century along with the box pews.

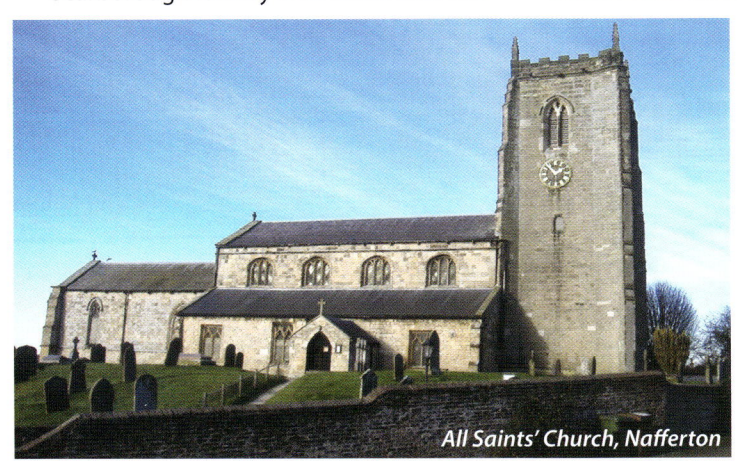

DO NOT turn left here, but walk straight ahead along this road which takes you to the parish Church of All Saints', Nafferton which stands at the side of the village school to your left.

All Saints' Church, Nafferton

19

DRIFFIELD to NAFFERTON

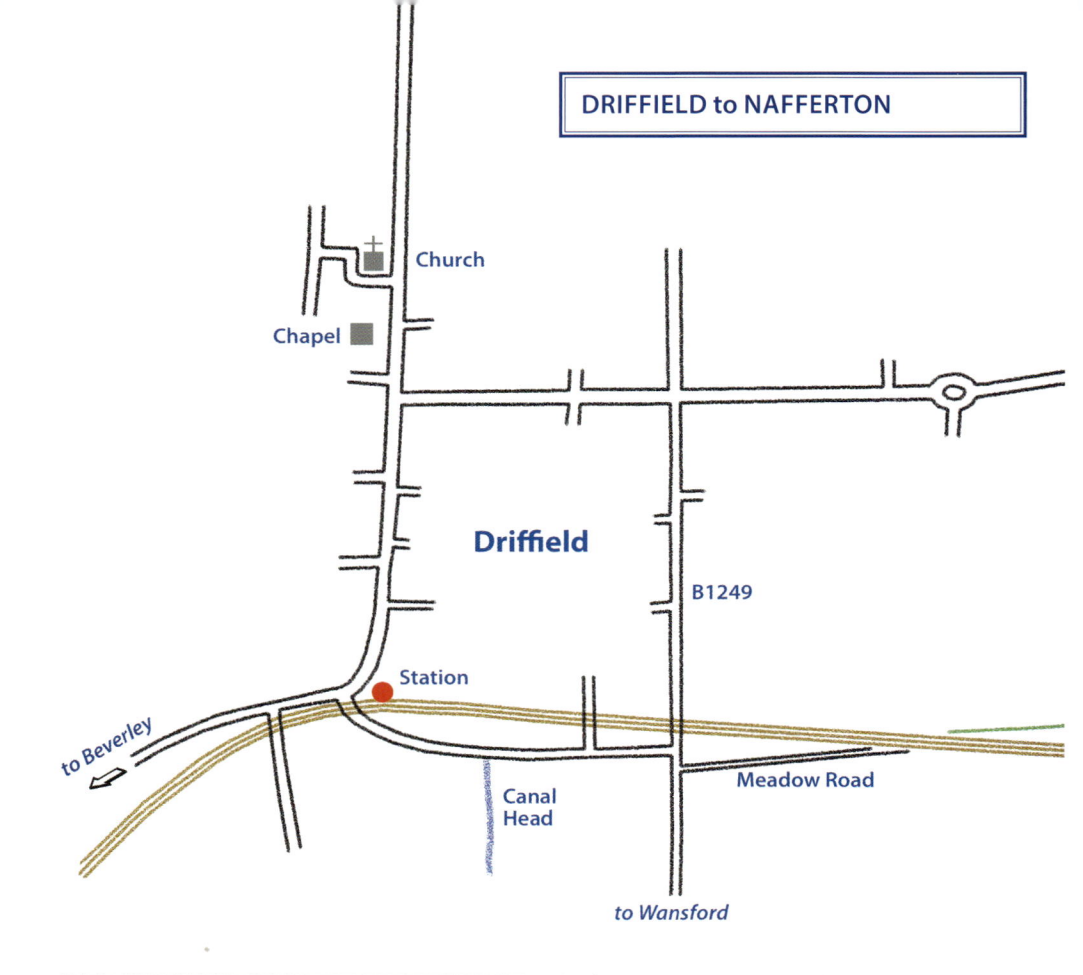

The 14th century Chancel of the Collegiate Church of St Martin is in ruins. The Nave has 13th century masonry and the lower part of the Tower is Perpendicular. There is a peculiar monument showing a couple beneath a sheet over which spreads a tree with branches which terminate in the heads of 13 children, it is probably mid 14th century.

After leaving the Church, walk along Coppergate, pass the village pond to your right and take the second left, Howe Lane, then first right onto Lowthorpe Lane. Follow this lane past the turkey farms before it turns into a track at Brickyard House. After two miles emerge onto the Lowthorpe road with St Martin's Church on the opposite side of the road, slightly to your left.

As you leave the Church, turn right onto the road for approximately 300yds. before turning right along a footpath on the edge of some trees. After passing the trees, walk in the direction of a footpath sign slightly to the right, aiming for the edge of some trees.

As you approach the end of these trees you will see a gate ahead. At the gate follow the track over a beck and alongside a farm

to Bridlington

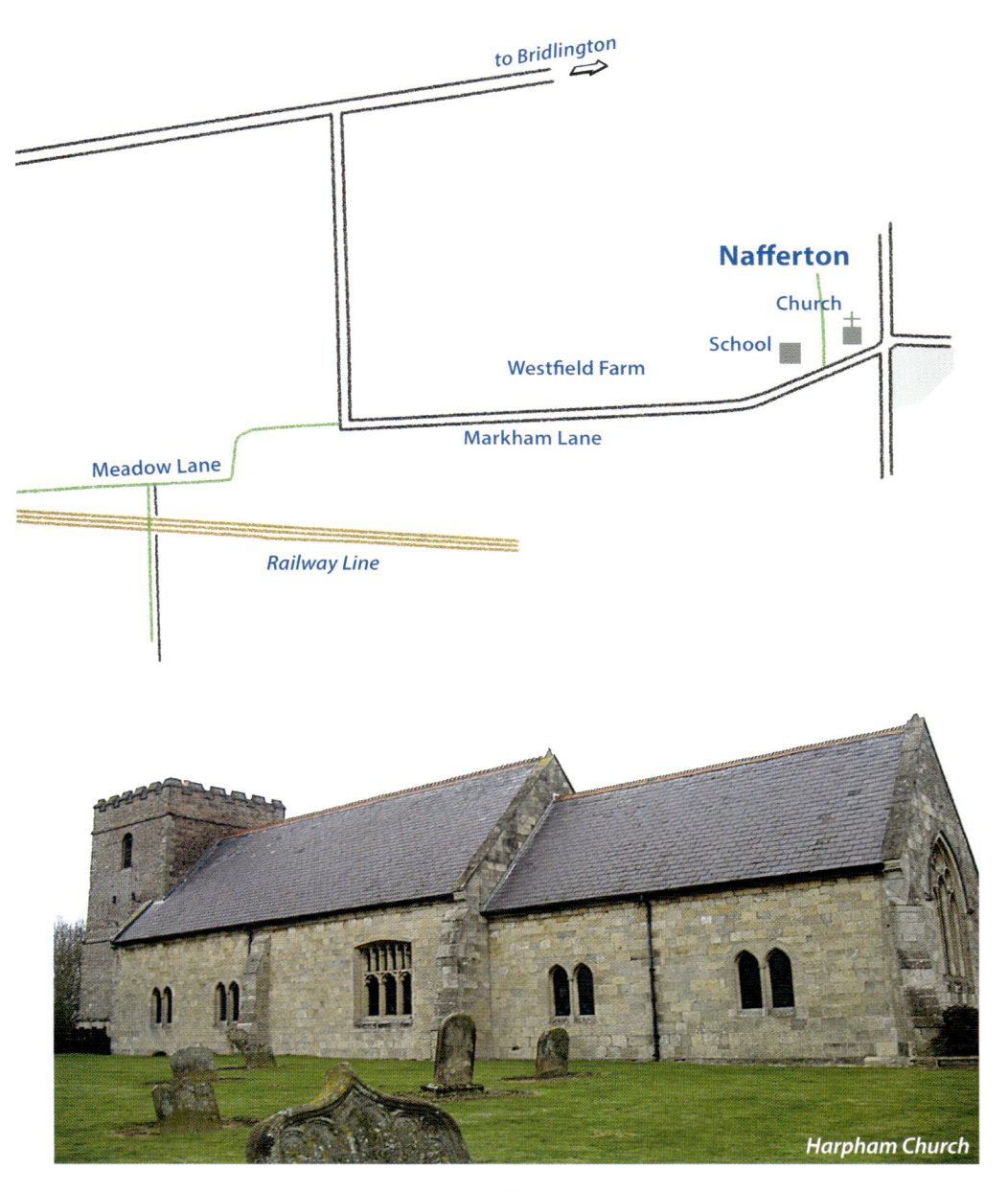

Nafferton
Church
School
Westfield Farm
Markham Lane
Meadow Lane
Railway Line

Harpham Church

Harpham Church chancel was built in 1827 and Temple Moore carried out a restoration before the great war. There are many Georgian fittings, also Heraldic Glass by William Peckitt of York. There are mediaeval monuments to the St Quentin family, including one of the finest brasses in Northern England, made around 1420.

NAFFERTON to HARPHAM

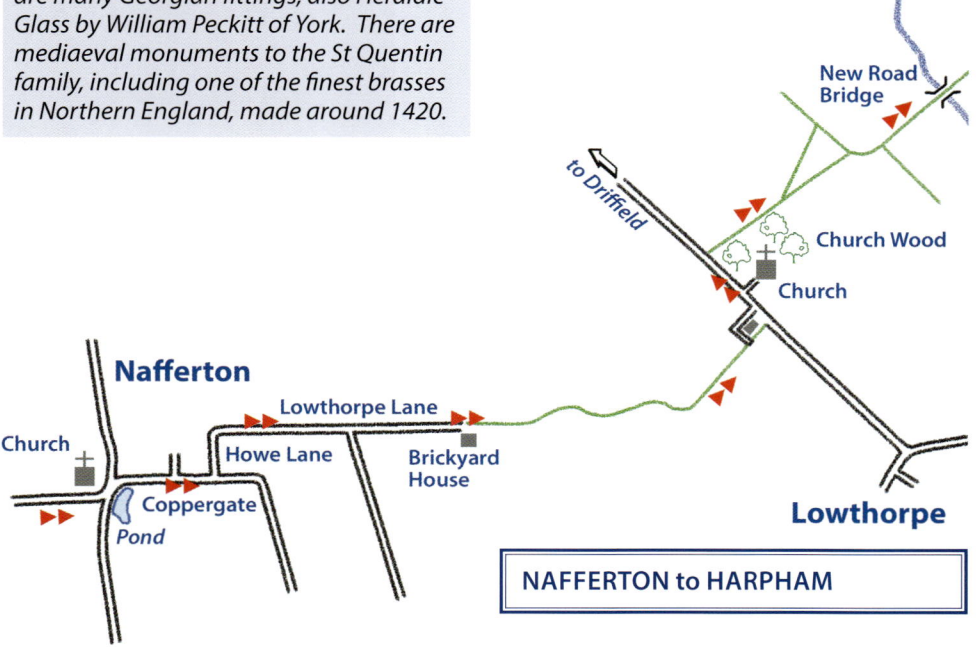

yard before emerging on to the Harpham – Kilham road. Turn right and follow this road into the village of Harpham, passing on your left St Quentin Arms. At the cross roads turn right into the cul-de-sac, you will see the Church to your right. St John of Beverley, the patron saint, is reputed to have been born in Harpham.

Having visited the Church, it is well worth visiting St John's Well, where it is reputed that St John of Beverley struck the ground with his staff and from that moment a spring emerged from the ground and still runs today. To reach St John's Well, return to the cross road and turn right, following the road as it bends left then right for 100yds. On your right you will come to the well which is protected by a metal cage.

Harpham is the conclusion of the second part of our journey.

We have covered 26 miles of the pilgrimage. The last leg of our journey heads for Kilham and along Woldgate.

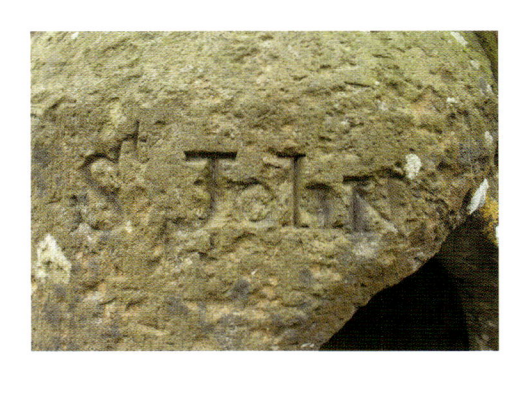

St John's Well, Harpham

23

FINAL LEG OF PILGRIMAGE
HARPHAM TO BRIDLINGTON

Distance: 10 miles

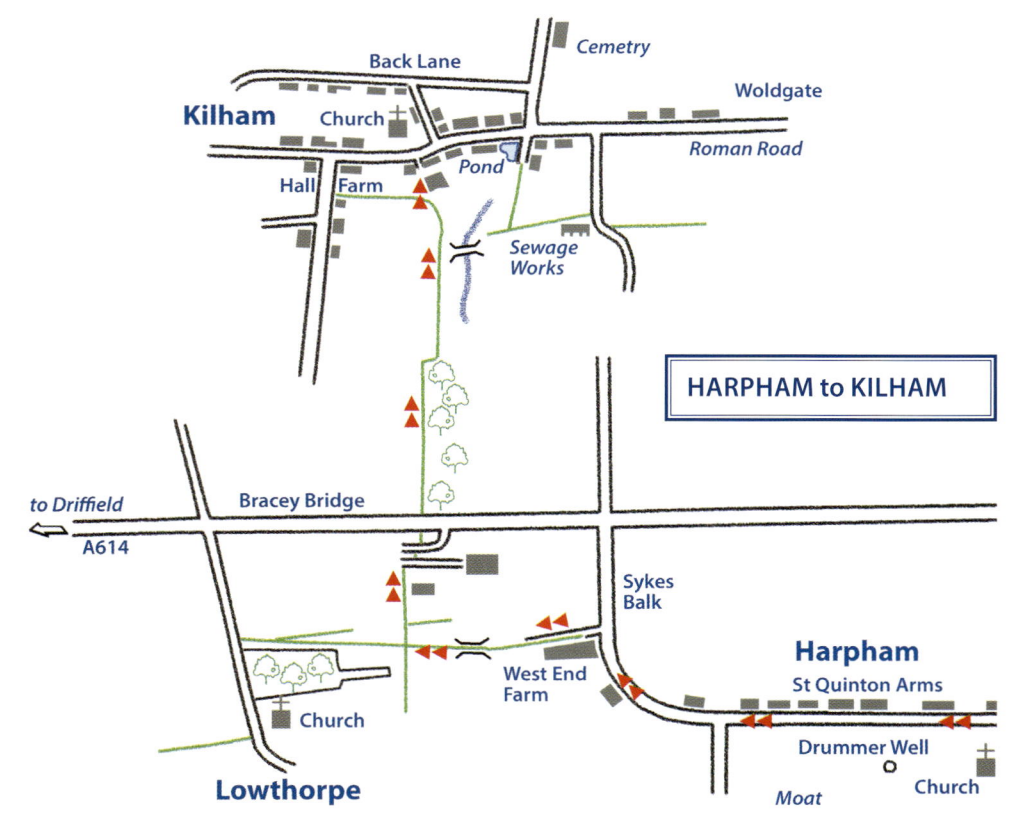

To continue the journey, return to the cross roads and walk along the main village street passing the St Quentin Arms on the right and Station Road on the left. Carry on round the bend passing Syke's Cottage and farm on the left. Soon there is a Public Bridleway on the left directing you along a rough access road to West End Farm. Keeping the farm to your left, go through an open gateway and take the track ahead. (This can be muddy and wet in winter or after heavy rain.) Walk along this track to arrive at a brick bridge over the clear waters of Lowthorpe Beck. Continue ahead passing sign posts under a tree on the left until further forward progress is barred by a metal gate. At this point, take the hand-gate beside the metal farm gate on the right. Continue in the same direction to cross the field, passing under

HARPHAM to KILHAM

24

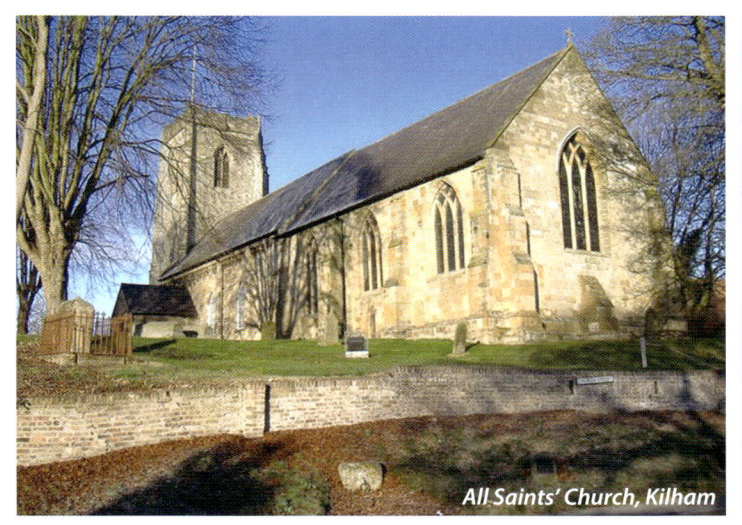

All Saints' Church, Kilham is well worth a visit. Apart from the 18th century windows, the Nave with its striking South Doorway is Norman. The Chancel dates from around 1300, and the Tower, although it incorporates some Norman carved stone, is Perpendicular. The Church also contains a Norman Font.

All Saints' Church, Kilham

overhead cables and head for a wooden hand-gate and signpost to the left of the hedging. Follow the sign-post for Bracey Bridge with an intermittent hedge on the left and open fields to the right, in the direction of farm buildings ahead. Follow the grassy track to a double metal farm gate and hand-gate to the left of the farm. A few yards ahead join the metalled farm road, and turn left away from the farm. Go through a wooden kissing gate alongside a metal farm gate into Bracey Bridge lay-by where refreshments may be available. On the opposite side of the lay-by and slightly to the right, is a picnic area. Follow the left hand edge of this to climb steps and go through a wooden gate to cross the busy A614 Bridlington-Driffield Road.

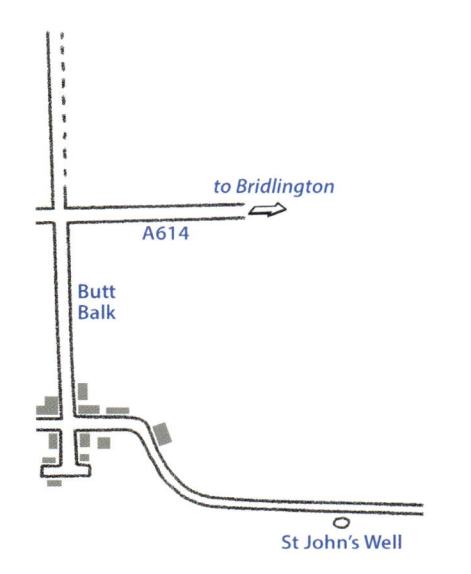

BRACEY BRIDGE TO KILHAM

This section is flat, but the path in the central section can be indistinct. The general direction is straight ahead and trees on your right and then a ditch on your right will help to keep you on track.

Cross this busy road with care, heading for a gap in the poles where a signpost indicates the way down the slope past an unused stile. Continue ahead along the path to the left of the trees emerging into a more open area. Bear slightly right to keep the trees close on your right hand side. Continue on this line, crossing a field boundary and, when the trees start to thin, again bear right for 20 yards to meet a ditch, turn left keeping the ditch on your right hand side.

This ditch will act as a faithful guide to lead you eventually very close to the church in Kilham. The path becomes clear as you cross several small fields, and the church tower appears ahead and slightly to the left. The path by the ditch leads under electric cables and to an open gateway with a ford, a brick bridge and sewage works to the right. Continue ahead to a barbed wire fence, under more electric cables, where the path swings to the left through an open gateway.

Go in the same direction for approximately 20 yards, then follow the track right, directly through the crop and follow the ditch around the edge of the field. Pass through a kissing gate to the right of Hall's Farm gate and enter Bakehouse Lane to come out opposite All Saints' Church. A few yards to your left is the Old Star Inn.

The majority of this section follows Woldgate. A Roman road, Woldgate is a quiet single track lane with passing places and although it undulates, there are no major climbs, there is a steady decent into Boynton.

Leaving the Church, turn left onto East Street and follow the road to pass the Post Office to the left and the Village pond to the right. Continue past the junction on your left following the road sign to Bridlington, 9 miles. Where the road bears right, (again signed Bridlington, 9 miles,) walk straight ahead entering Woldgate. After approximately 1½ miles, Tuft House farm is passed on your left, followed by two lanes to your right for Burton Agnes. After the second turning to your right there is a turn to Rudston on your left. Continue for ¾ mile to pass a metal radio mast to your left, and a further 1¼ miles brings you to a crossroads with Carnaby to the right. Continue straight ahead with Sands Wood to the left. When the trees of Sands Wood end you will see a gap about 200 metres on the left before you

KILHAM to BOYNTON

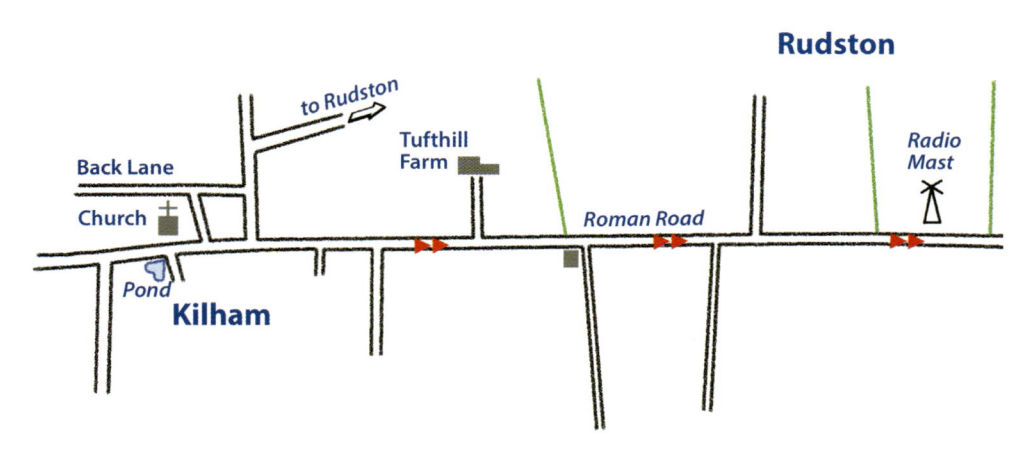

reach another smaller belt of woodland, now on both sides of the road. There is a bridleway sign off to the right and a broad chalky farm track beyond a metal barrier on the left.

From here there are two ways to return to the Priory Church: (a) to carry straight on along Woldgate turning left at the 'T' Junction, or, (b), which we would suggest, enabling you to visit St Andrew's Church, Boynton. To take this route, turn left at the metal barrier and follow the chalk farm road heading downhill through the trees. After a while the asymmetrical towers of Bridlington Priory may be seen through the gaps in the right hand hedgerow. The view opens up when the buildings of Home Farm are reached on the right. The farm track bears left over a brick bridge spanning Gypsey Race and enters another short stretch of woodland. Soon some houses appear and a blue marker indicates the way ahead, the track bears right to reach the road opposite the church.

The Turkey Lectern

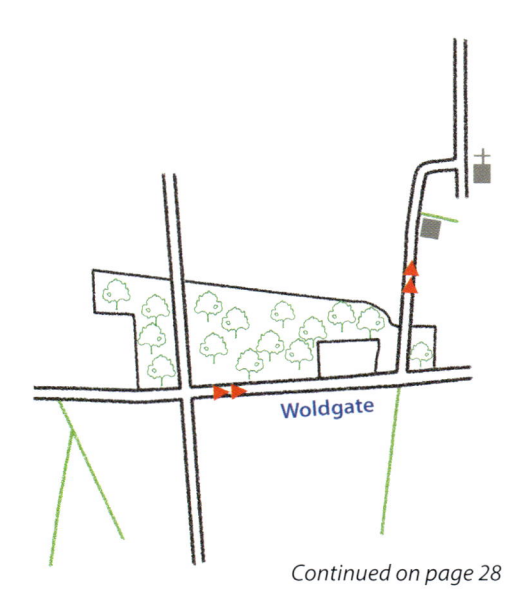

Continued on page 28

27

BOYNTON to BRIDLINGTON PRIORY

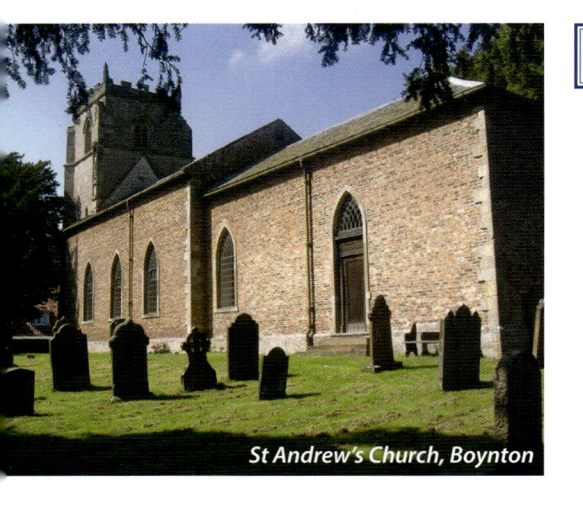

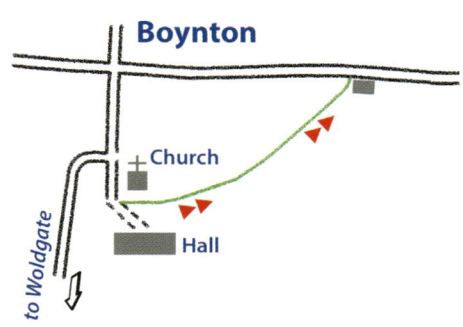

St Andrew's Church, Boynton

St Andrew's Church stands on the southern edge of the village, where the road ends at the gates of Boynton Hall, home of the Strickland family for more than four centuries. The fine Georgian house to the north of the Church is the old vicarage, the last vicar to live there retired at the end of the second world war. The Tower was added to the Church in the first half of the 15th century.

There is a West window in the Perpendicular style of that period, which gives light to the first floor gallery, above that is the bell chamber which today houses two bells. The Tower was the only part of the mediaeval church to survive an extensive rebuilding in the middle years of the 18th century. Tradition has it that the old church was destroyed in a fire. New research has shown that this was not the case The church gradually fell into disrepair and by 1769 parts had collapsed. At the end of the Nave stands the unique double Chancel screen of two responds and two quatrefoil columns, with Gothic capitals and Classical architrave. This arrangement is repeated one bay further on to form an architectural baldacchino for the altar. Beyond the Chancel lies the Strickland Mortuary Chapel separated from the rest of the church by an iron railing.

You may also be interested to visit the grave of John Stephenson, Sir George Strickland's shepherd, which is situated right up against the south wall of the churchyard. Boynton's most photographed treasure is the famous "Turkey Lectern". The lectern was designed by local architect F.F. Johnson, and carved by the Boynton craftsman Harry Scott. The colourful font cover of 1950 was also designed by him.

The last section is flat and should be easy to follow. After an enclosed pretty path there is a section of the B1253 to walk before some street walking in Bridlington to arrive at the Priory.

Follow the footpath sign to the left of Boynton Hall gate through a gap in the wall to take a path enclosed between the churchyard on the left and the metal fence of Boynton Hall on the right.

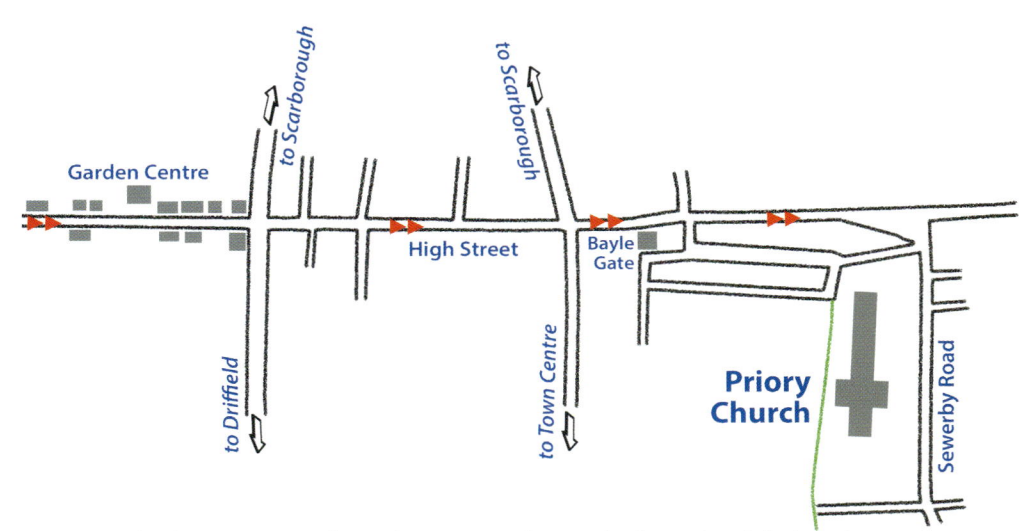

A stream/ditch appears on the right and accompanies the clear path before giving way to a wooden fence on the right and recent tree plantings on the left. The modern buildings of Beachbrook are passed on the right and a short gravel path leads through an area of new planting. The path then becomes enclosed with hedging to the left and broken fencing to the right and runs parallel to a tarmac drive on the right before bearing left over 100 yards of rough ground to emerge onto the B1253 at the side of a white bungalow. Turn right and, with care, take the narrow footpath along the right hand grass verge. Pass Easton Farm on the left and after a 30 mph sign, Eastfield Garden Centre is on the left. Shortly the narrow footpath can be abandoned for a broader pavement on the left and the busy A165 road is reached. Cross with care and head for the gap in the poles where a footpath leads past a Bretel Walk sign and on to Westgate. Continuing in the same direction go straight ahead down High Street. At the traffic lights cross the road carefully and continue along Bayle Gate where you will be greeted by the magnificent sight of Bridlington Priory.

THE COUNTRY CODE

When walking in the country always remember that many depend on it for their livelihood. The Country Code reminds us the rules to be observed when out for a country walk.

1. Guard against the risk of fire
2. Fasten all gates
3. Keep dogs under proper control
4. Avoid damaging fences, hedges and walls
5. Keep to the path across farm land
6. Leave no litter, take it home with you
7. Safeguard water supplies
8. Protect wild life, wild plants and trees
9. Go carefully on country roads
10. Respect the life of the countryside

PRIORY 900
1113 - 2013

This walk takes place in three stages – starting at Beverley Minster to be walked over three days – approximately 36 miles

Church Bridlington

9781326716707